Reading Program 〔 Book 2: or 〕

Good Sports

by Francie Alexander
Illustrated by Jim Durk

Based on the books by
Norman Bridwell

SCHOLASTIC INC.
New York   Toronto   London   Auckland   Sydney
Mexico City   New Delhi   Hong Kong   Buenos Aires

It was a nice morning.

"I want to go to the seashore," said Cleo.

"Good idea!" said Clifford.

"Here we go!" said T-Bone.

On the way to the shore, the dogs heard a horn. Cleo jumped in surprise and stepped on a thorn.

"Do you want to stop?" asked T-Bone.

"No, I want to go to the shore," said Cleo.

"You are a good sport," said Clifford.

On the way to the shore,
the dogs saw a fort.
They smelled popcorn
and they heard the ferry
blow its horn.

"What a fun day!"
said Clifford.

Gray clouds started
to form.

Clifford gave Cleo and
T-Bone a lift.
They raced home away
from the storm.

"Thanks, Clifford,"
said Cleo.

"You are a good sport,"
said T-Bone.

When they got to
Clifford's home,
Emily Elizabeth said,
"Come on, get out
of the storm!"

"Is our fun day over?"
T-Bone asked.

"No!" said Clifford. "We
will find more fun inside."

She invited them in
for s'mores.

The dogs went inside and
had even more fun.